Wasteland

coloring book

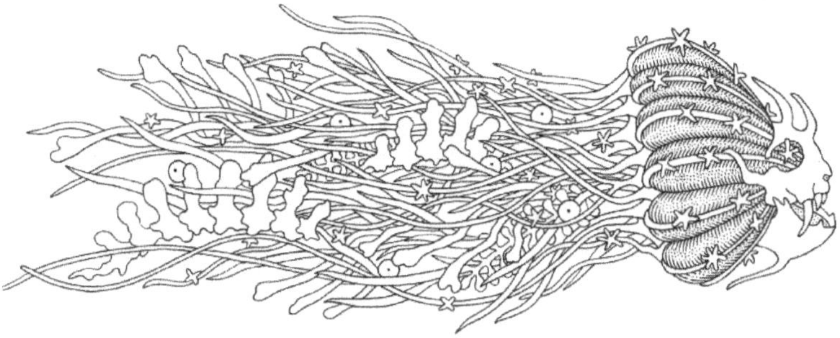

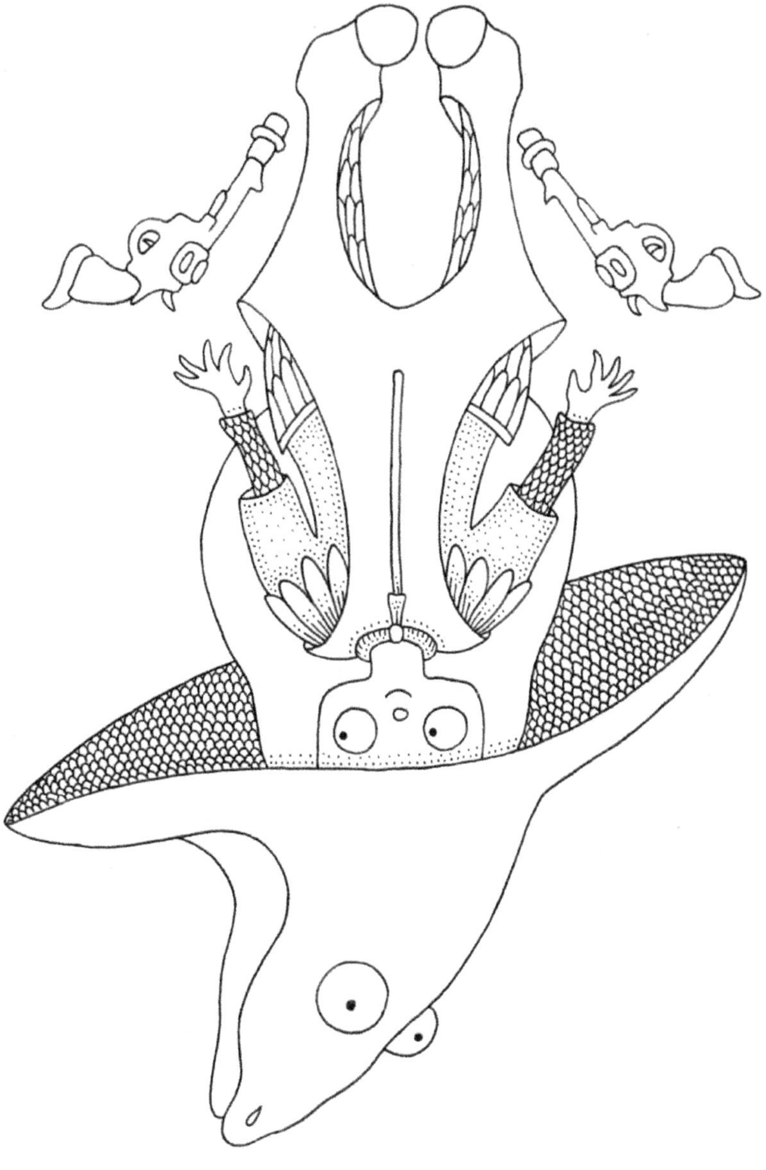

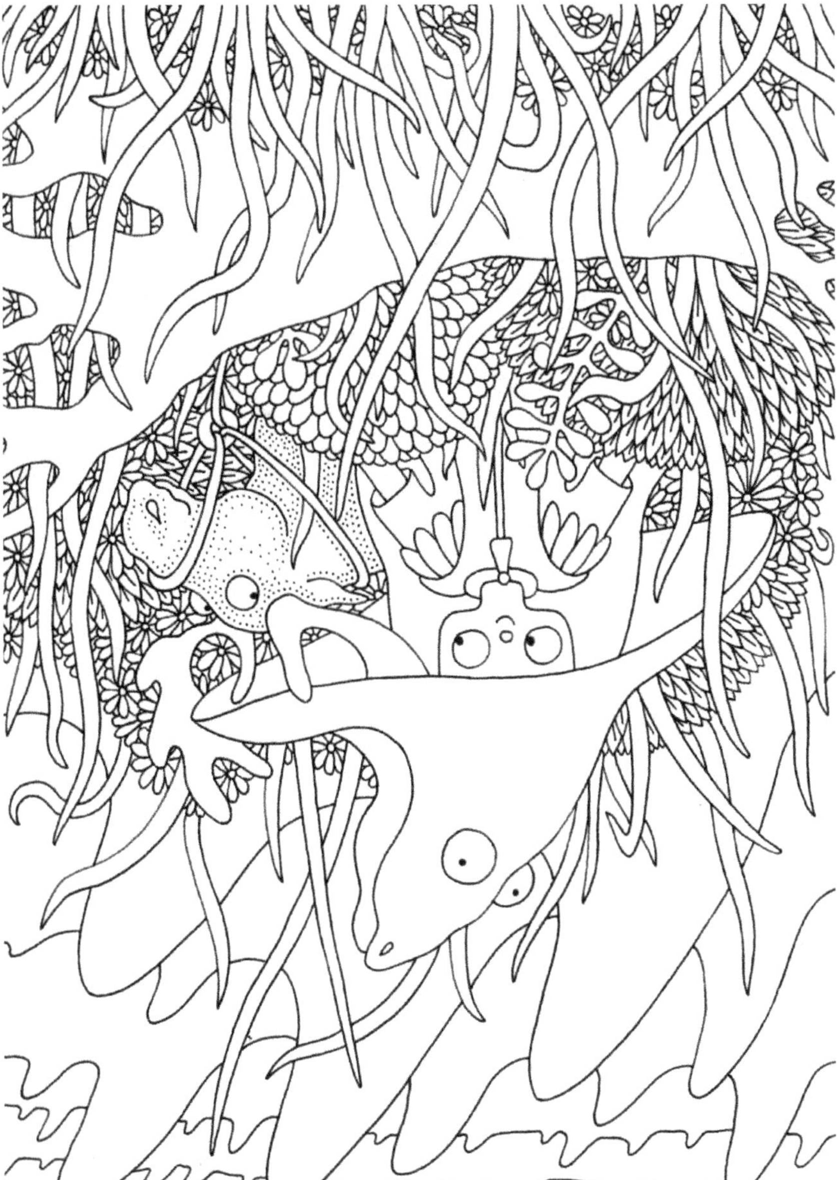

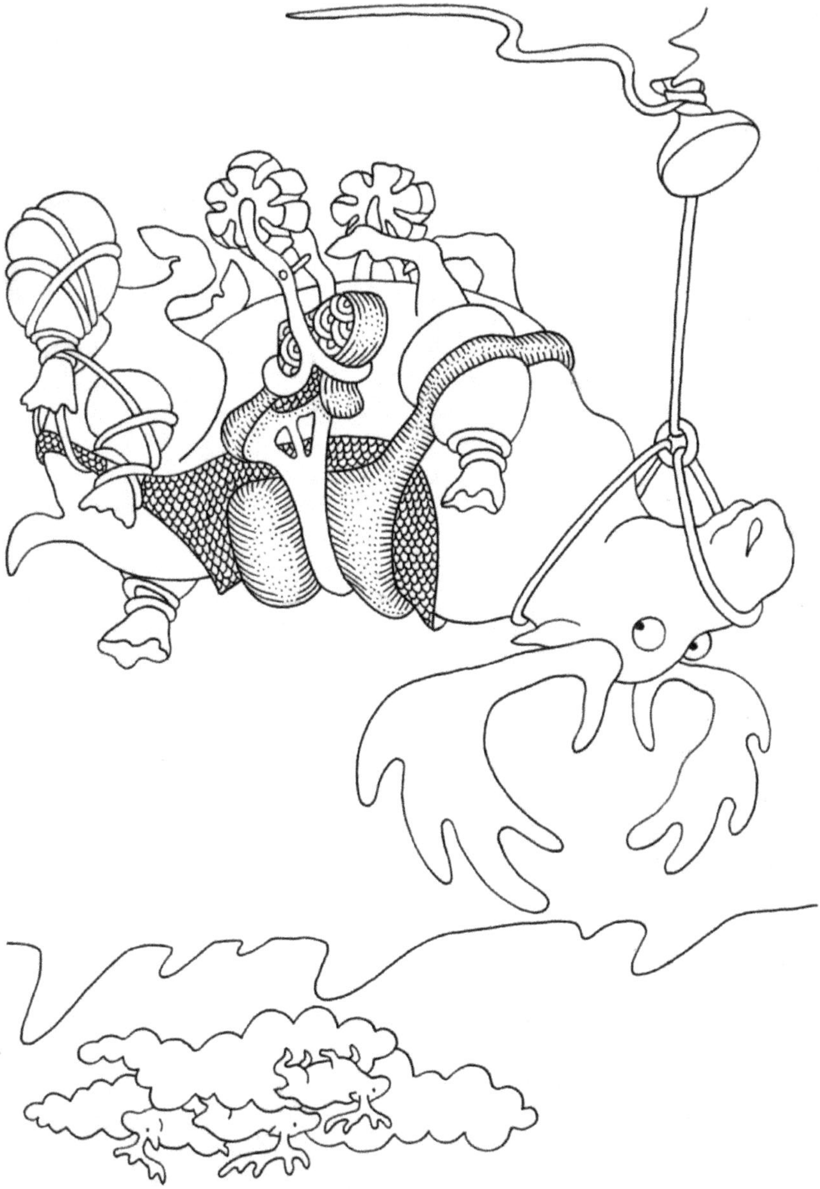

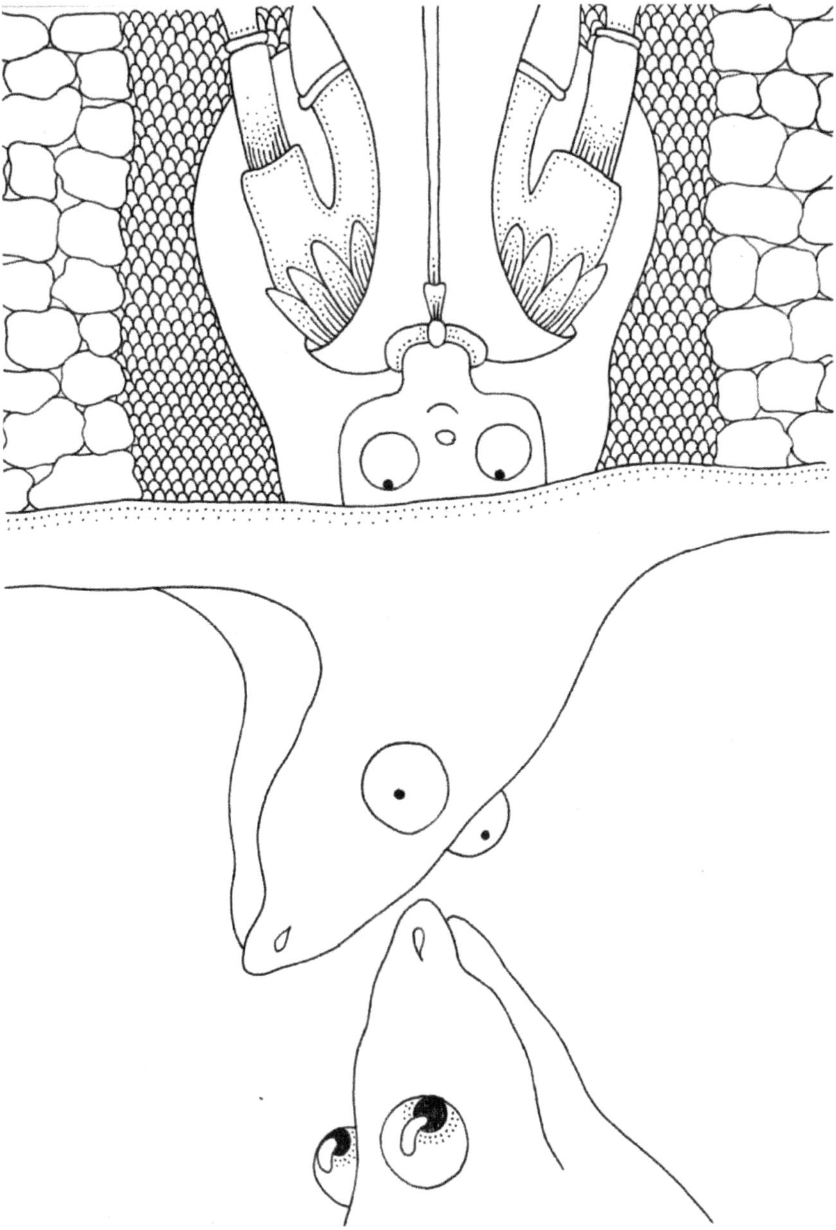

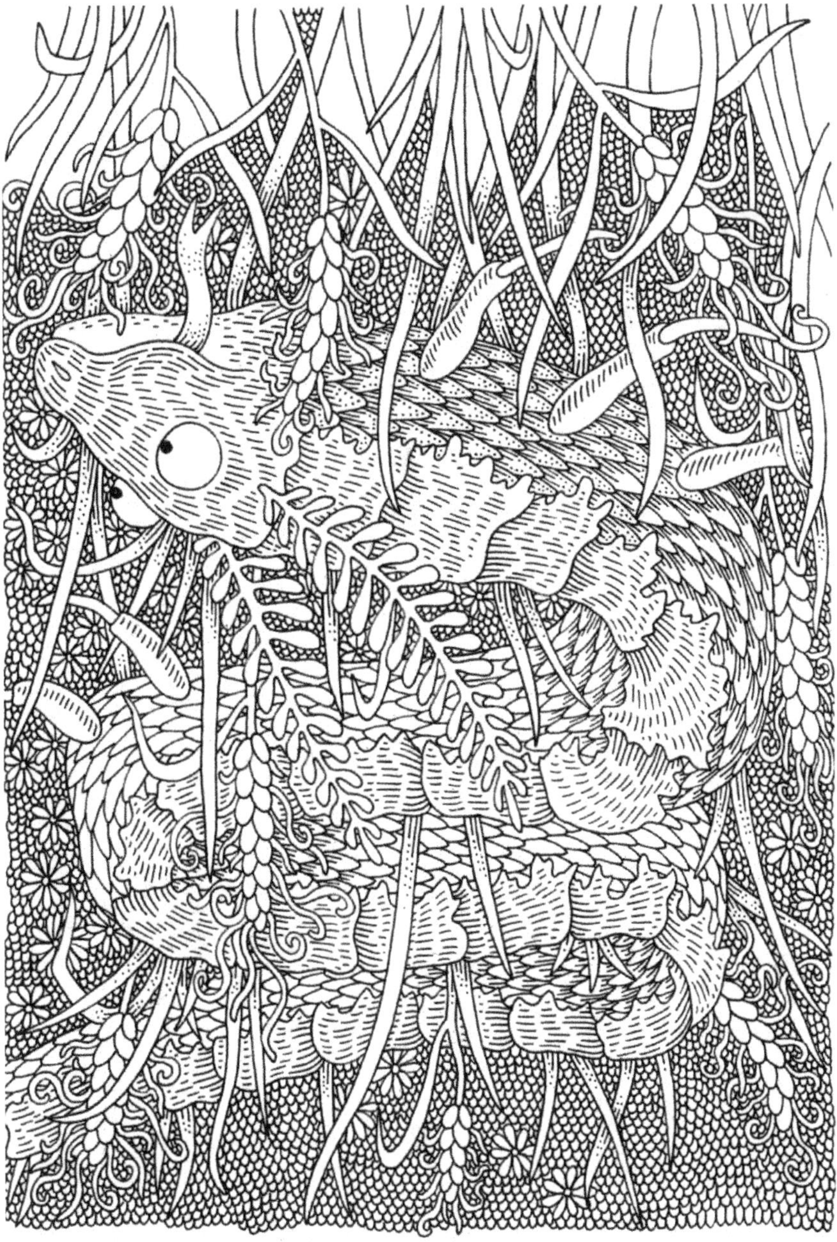

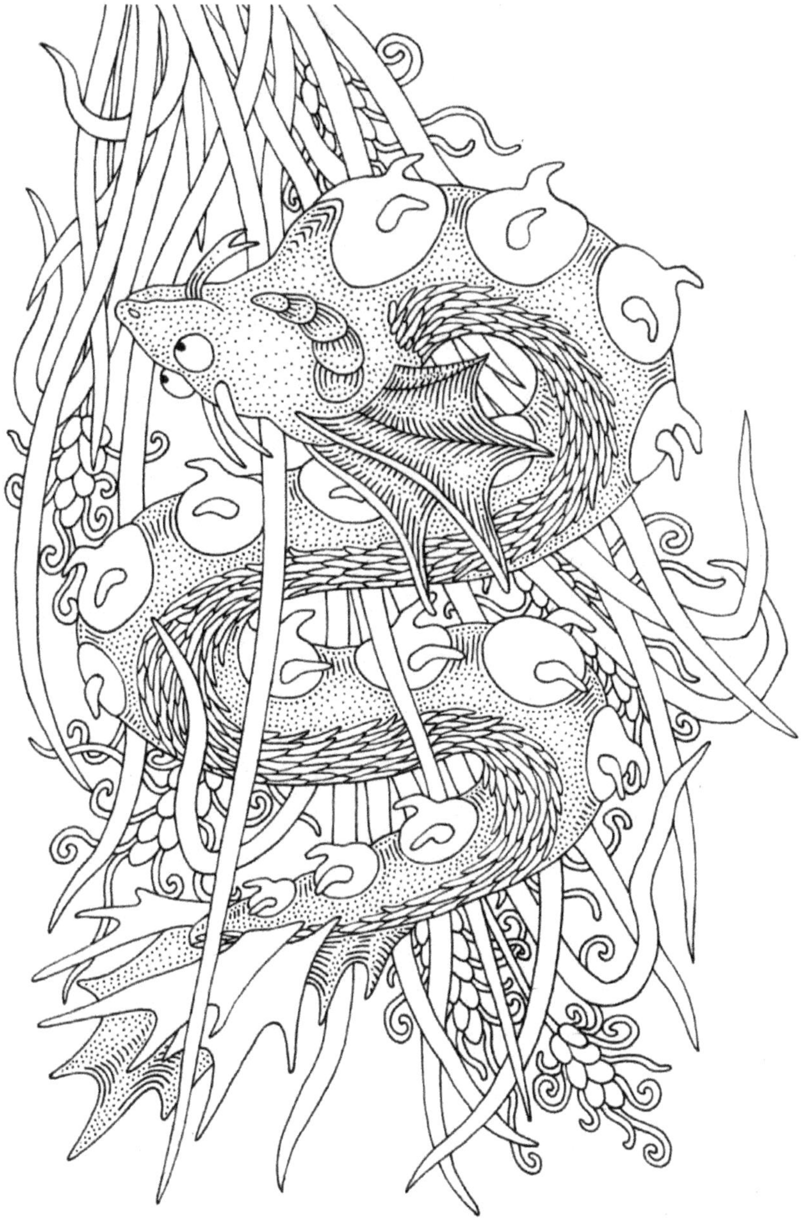

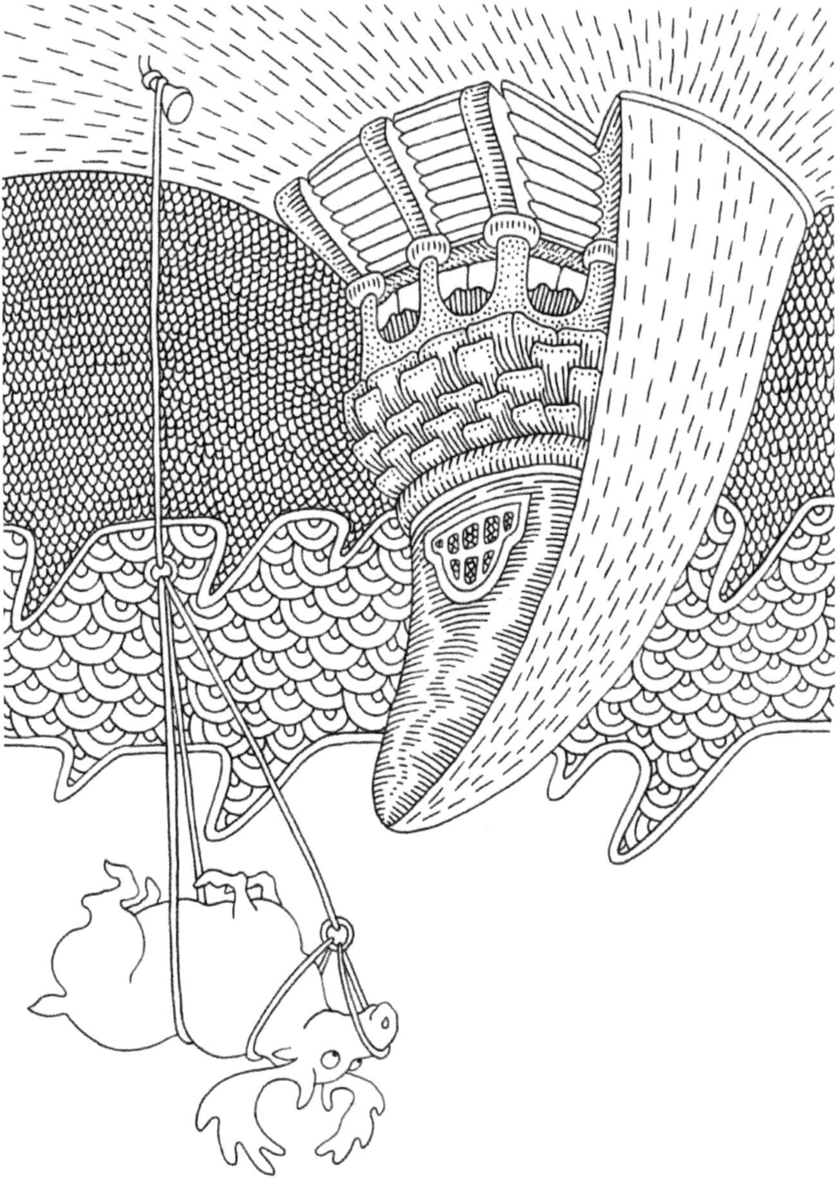

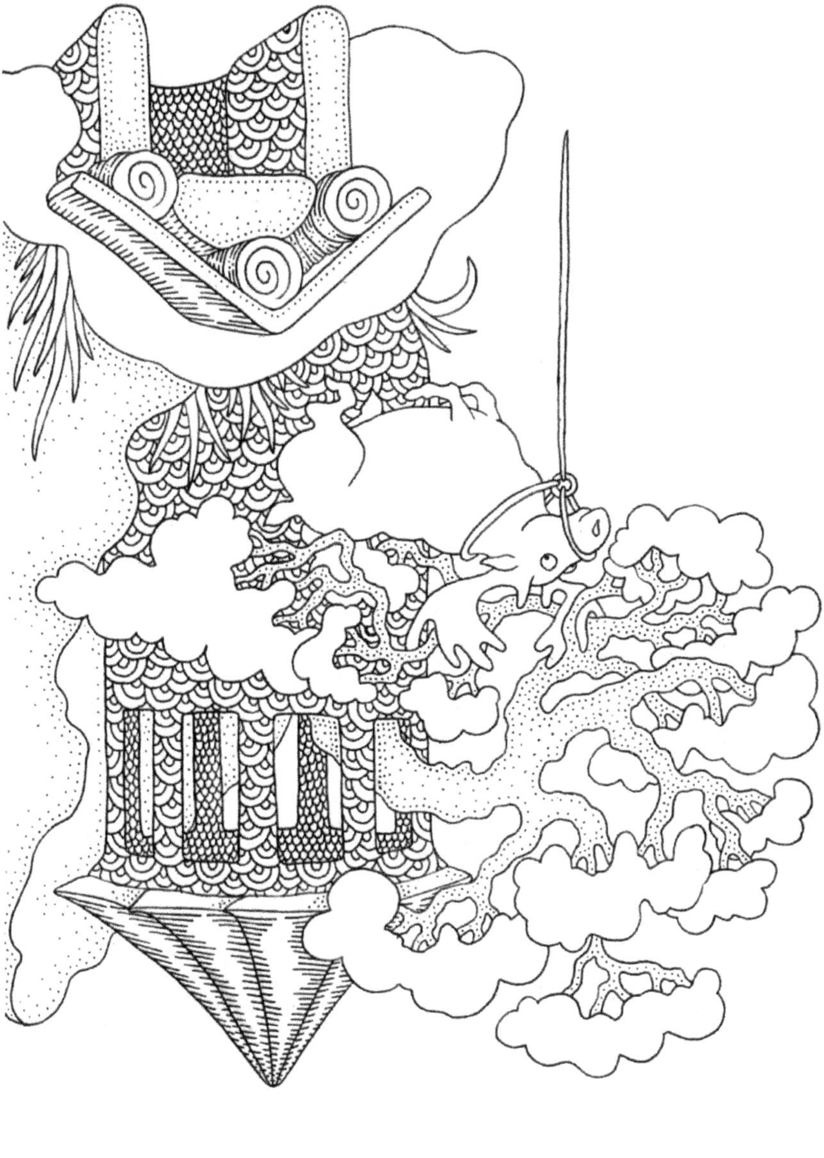

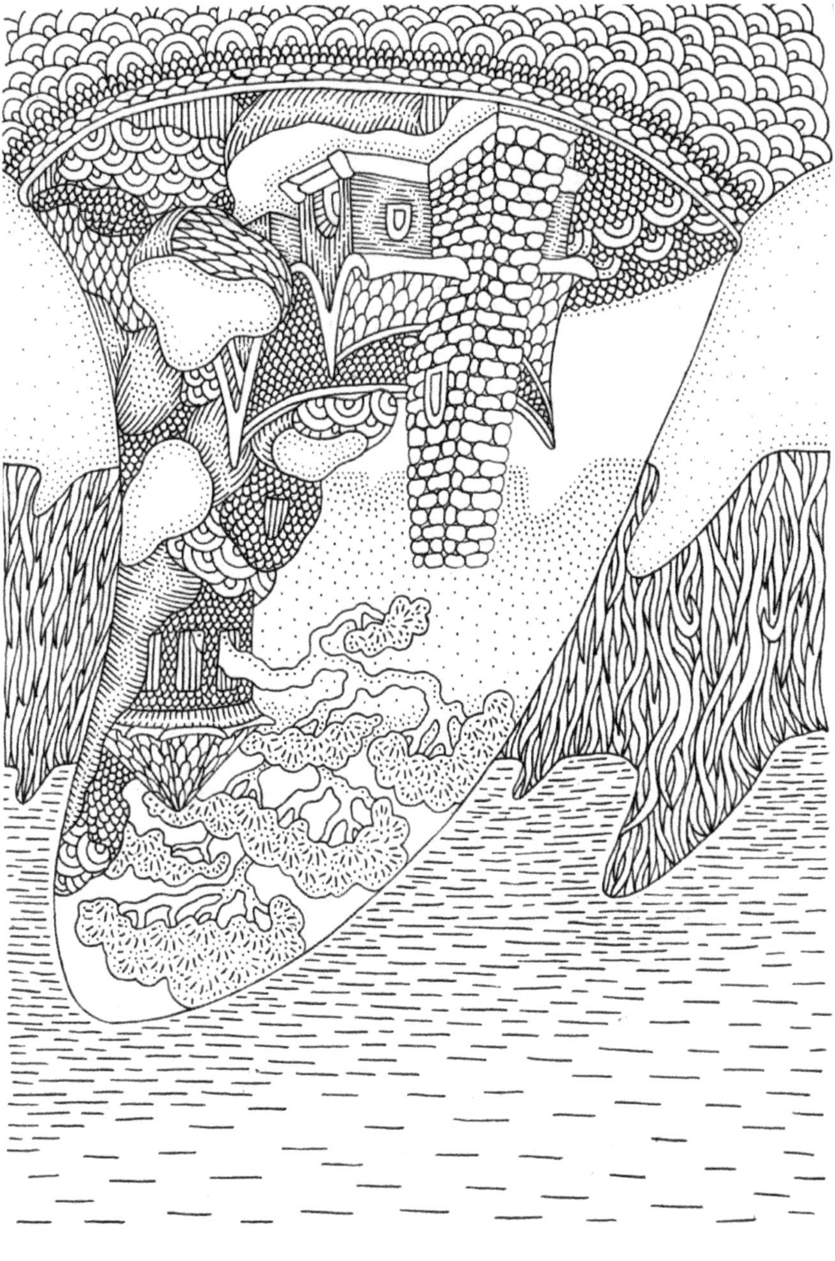

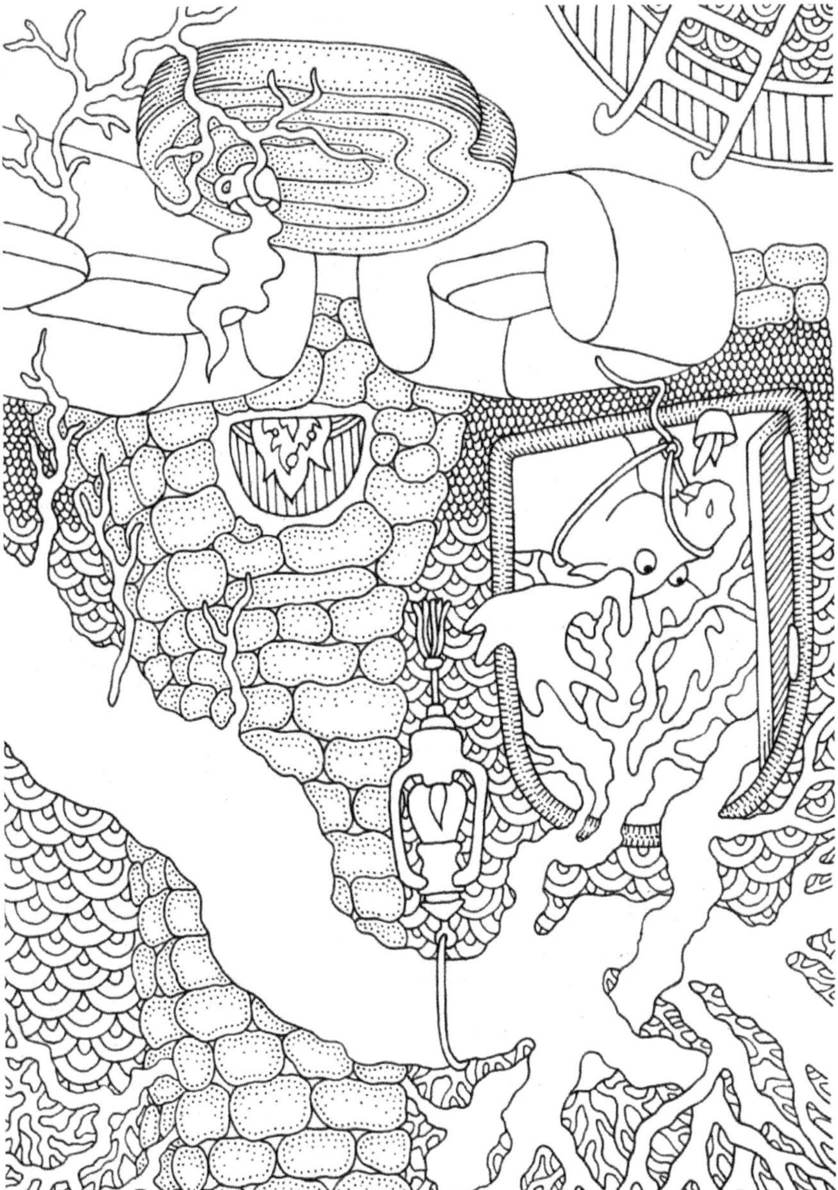

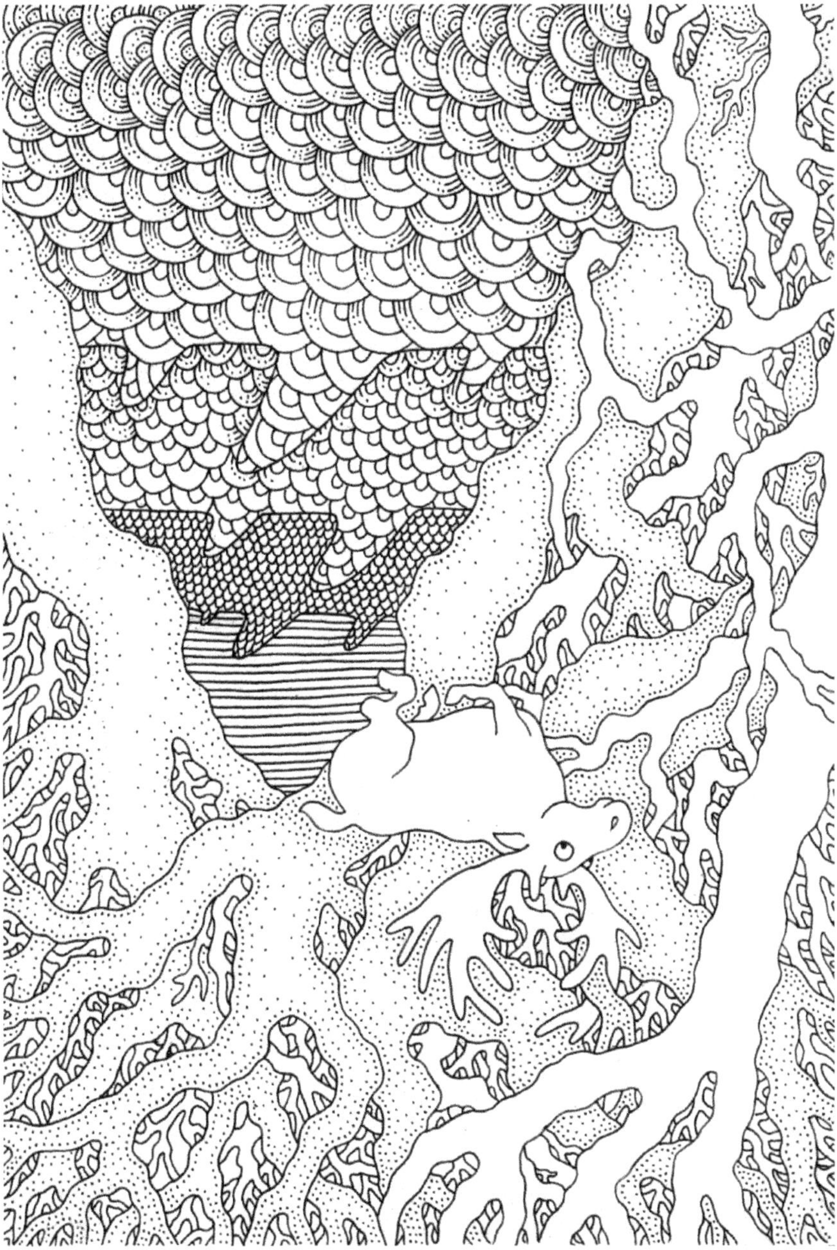

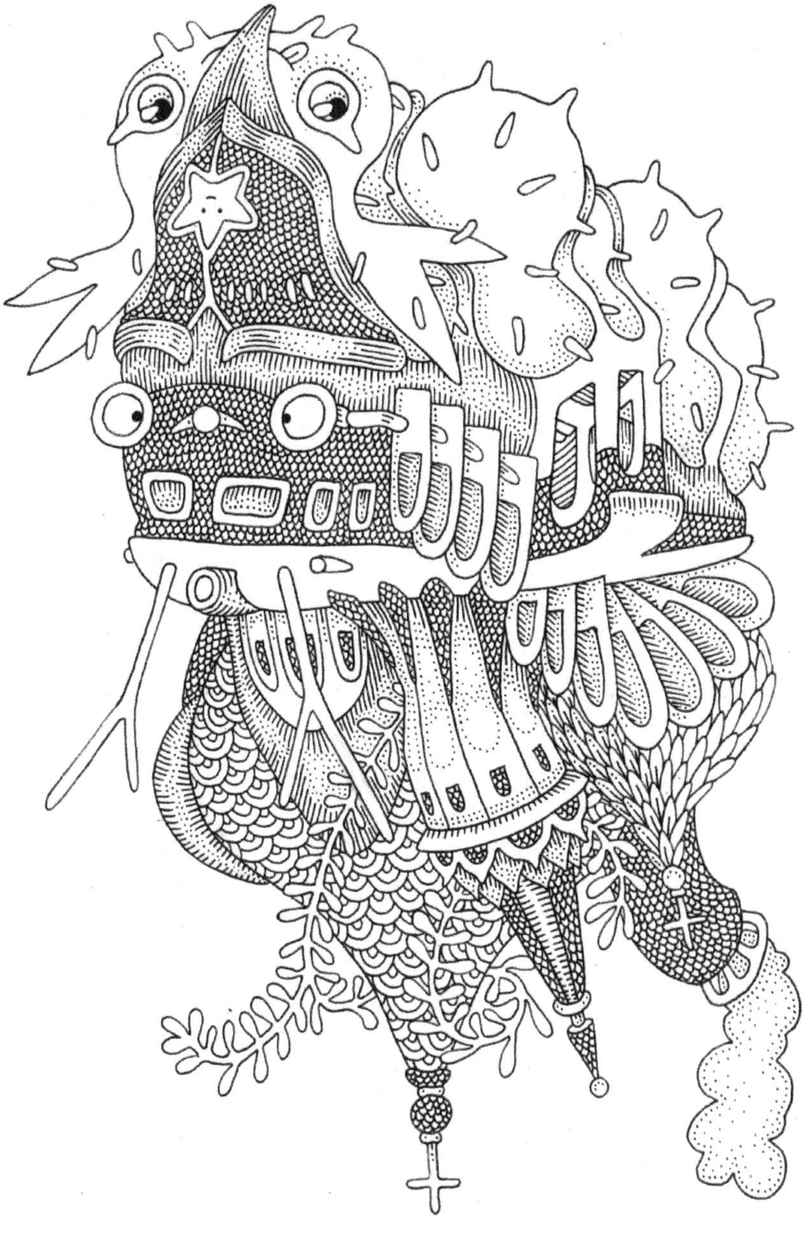

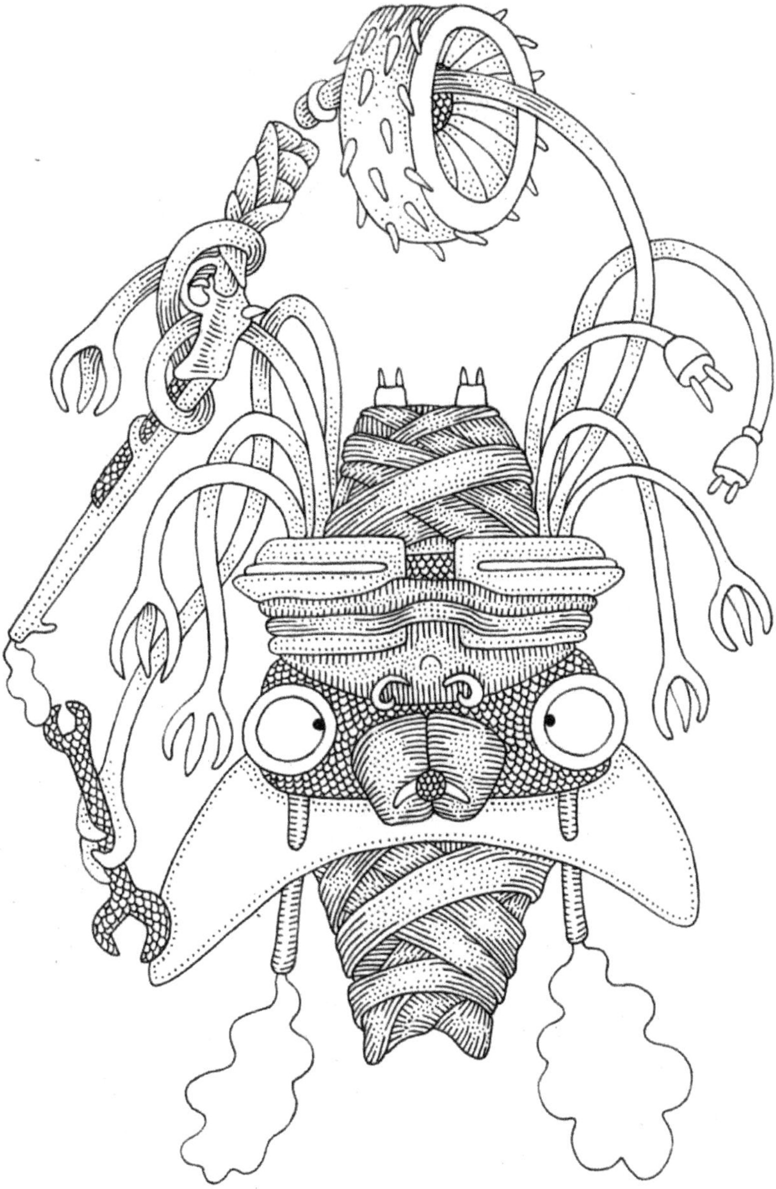

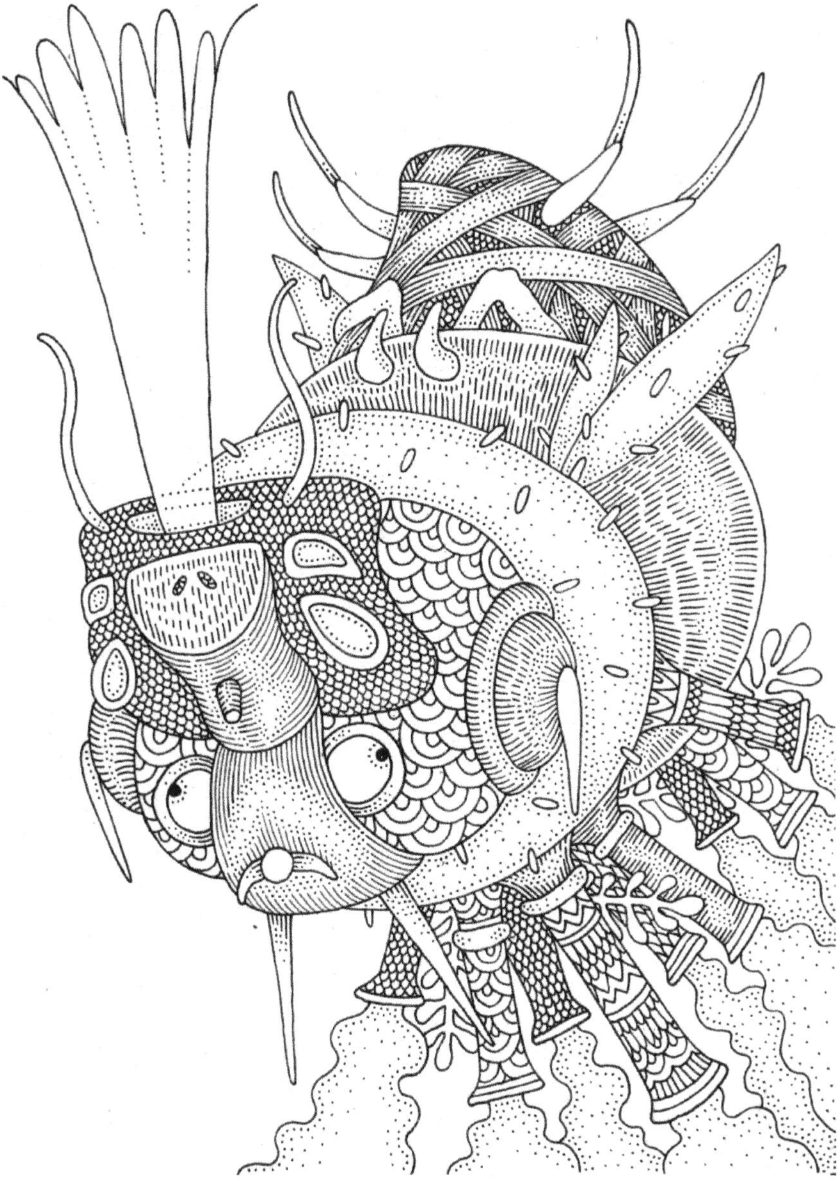

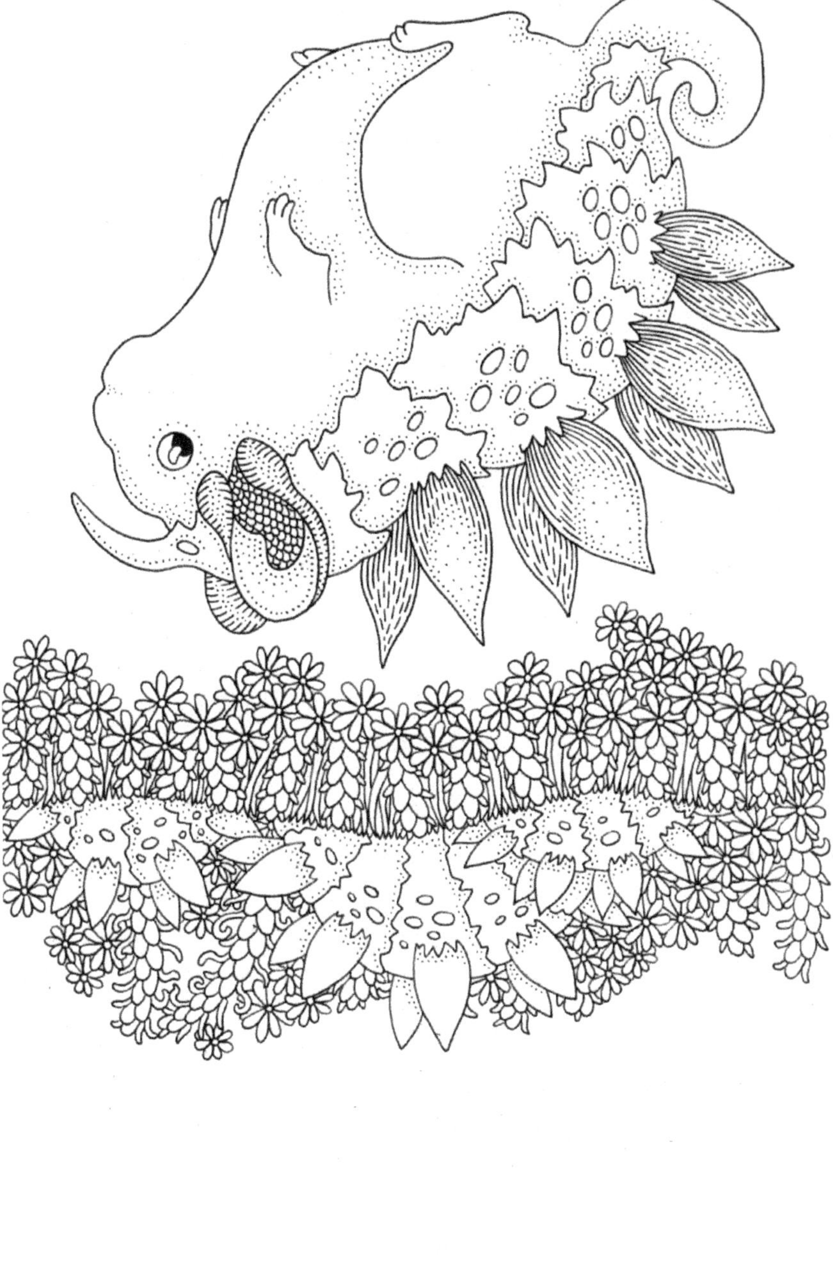

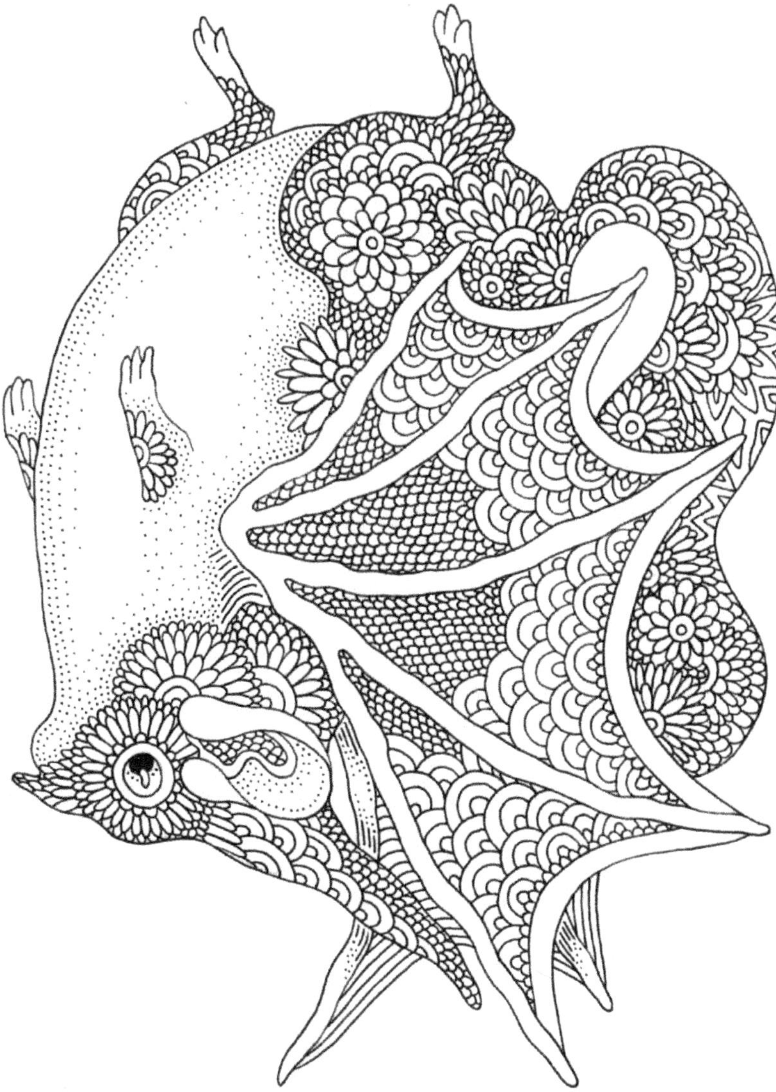

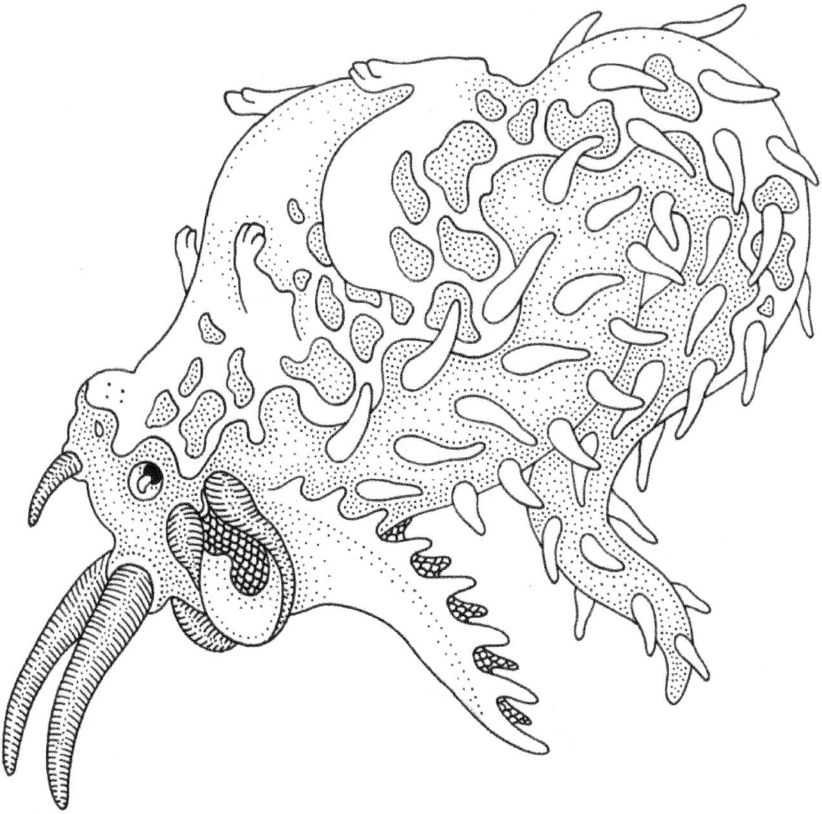

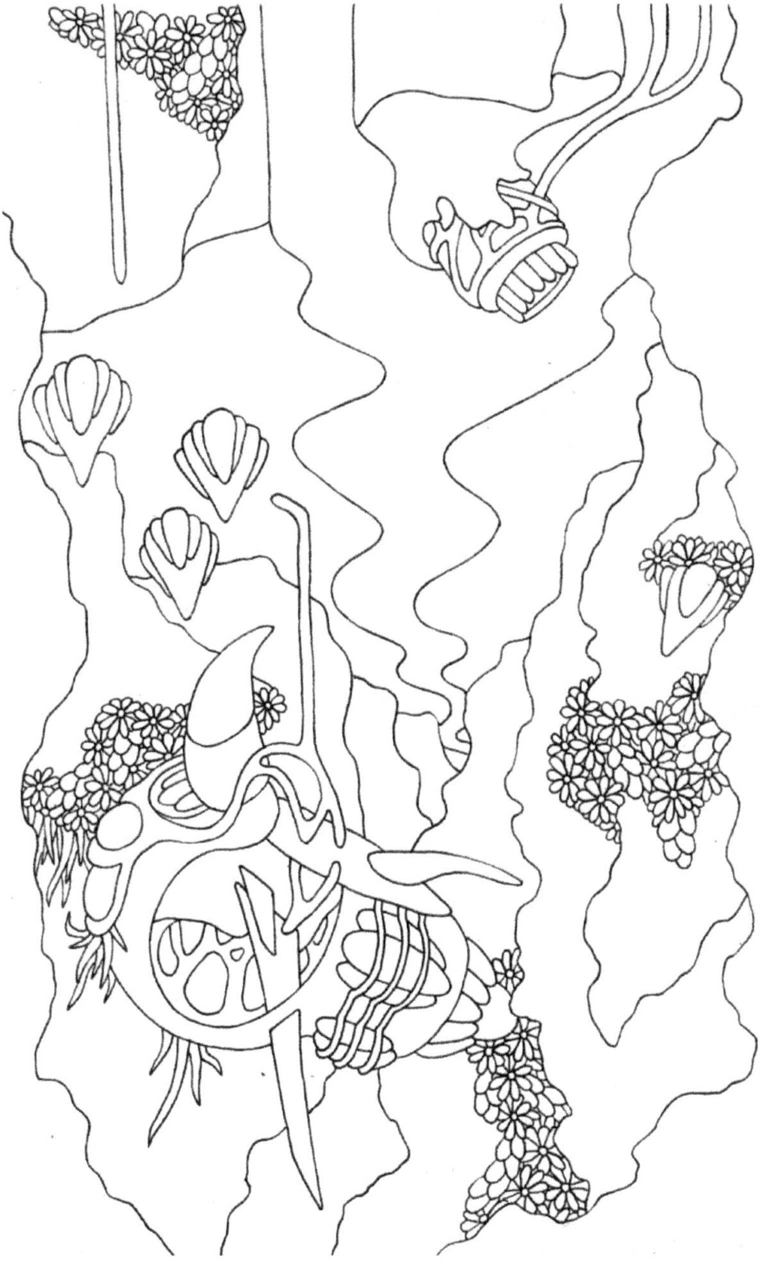

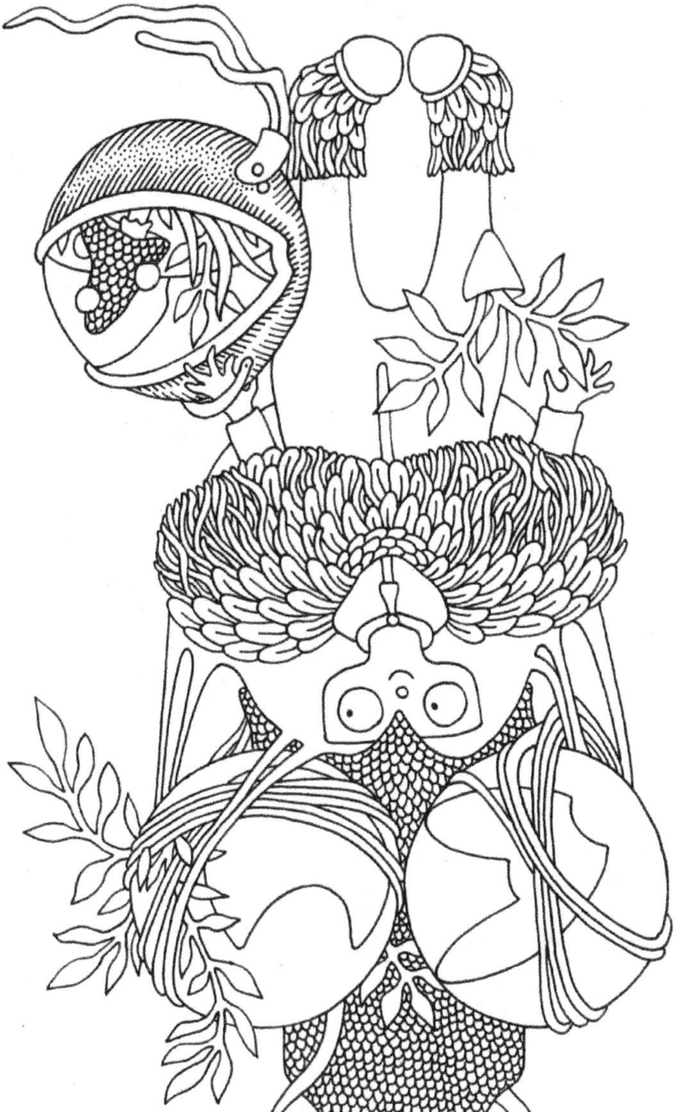

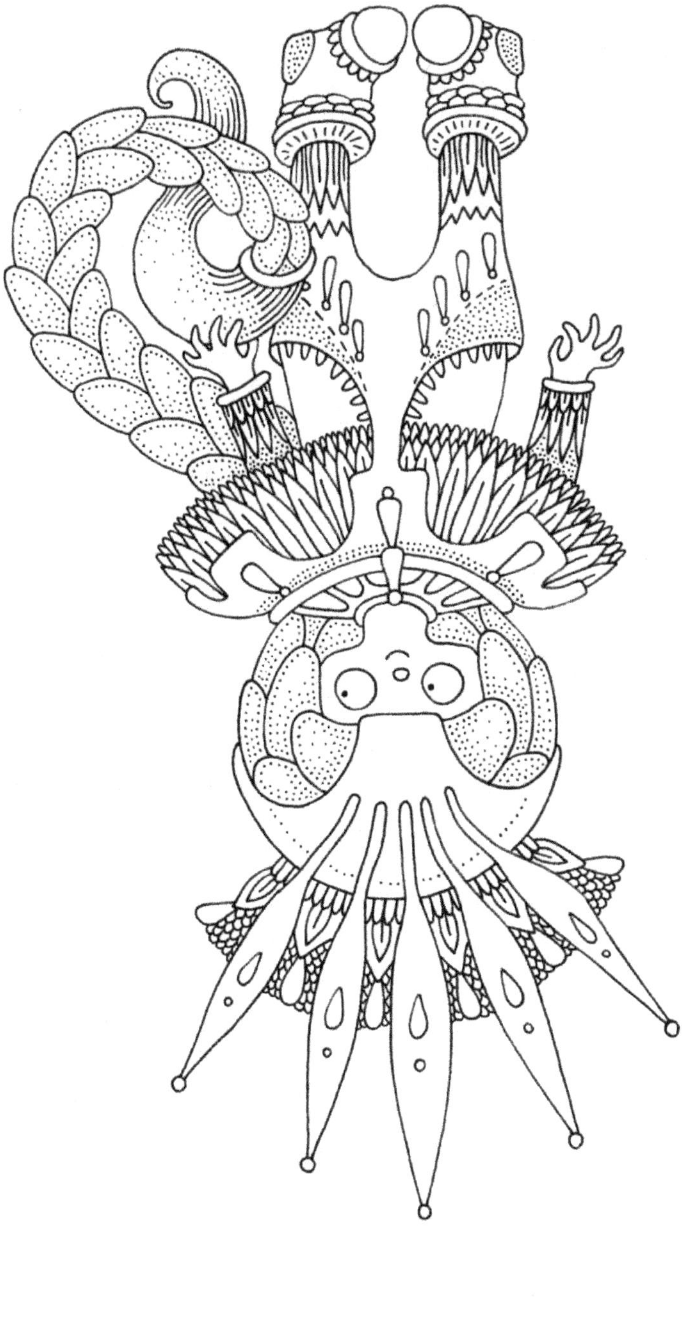

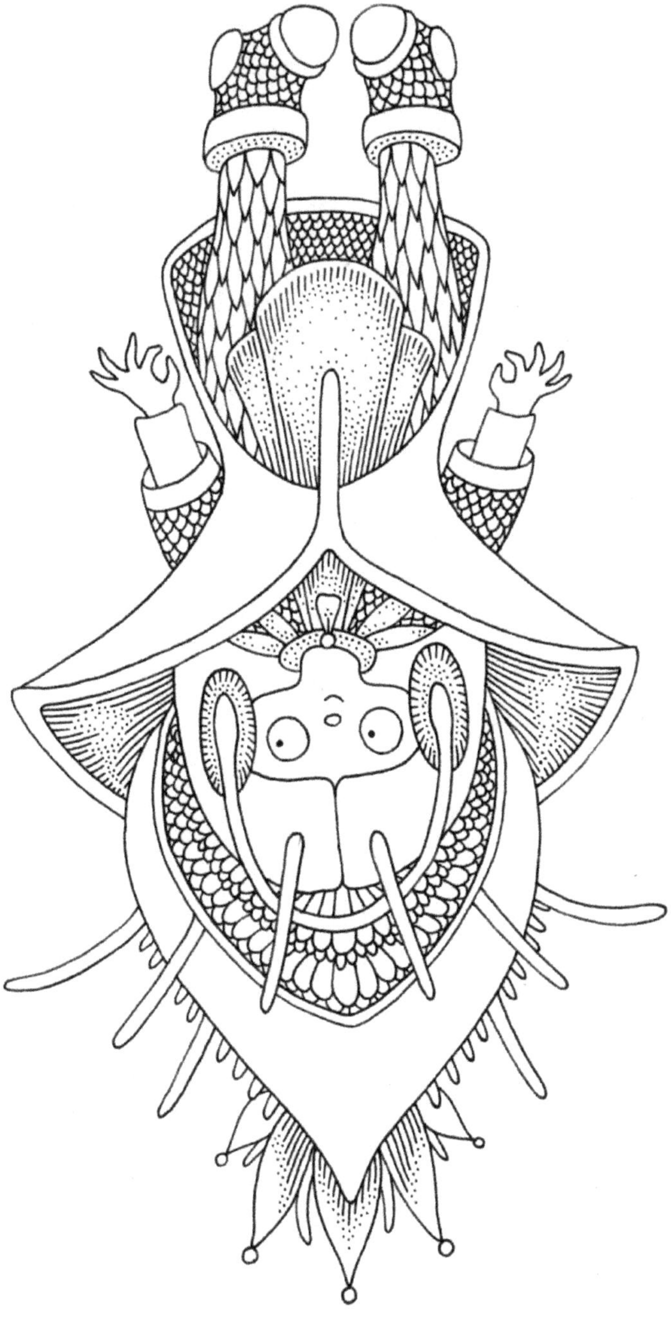

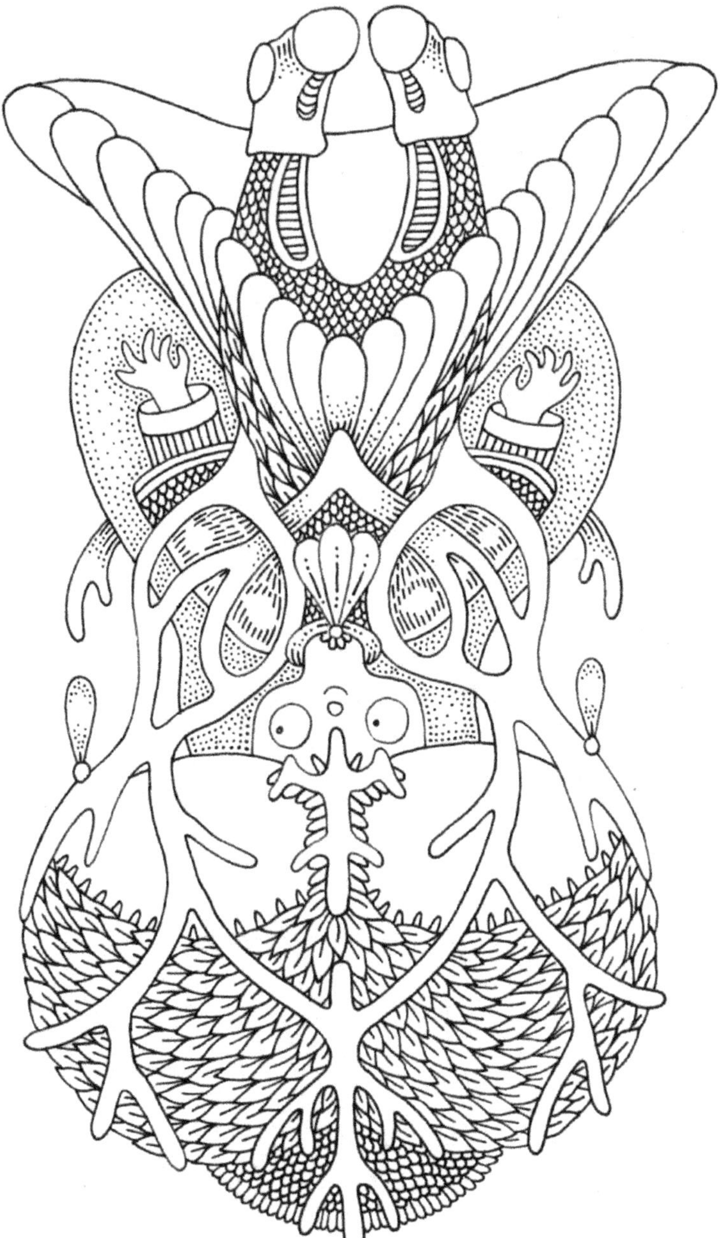

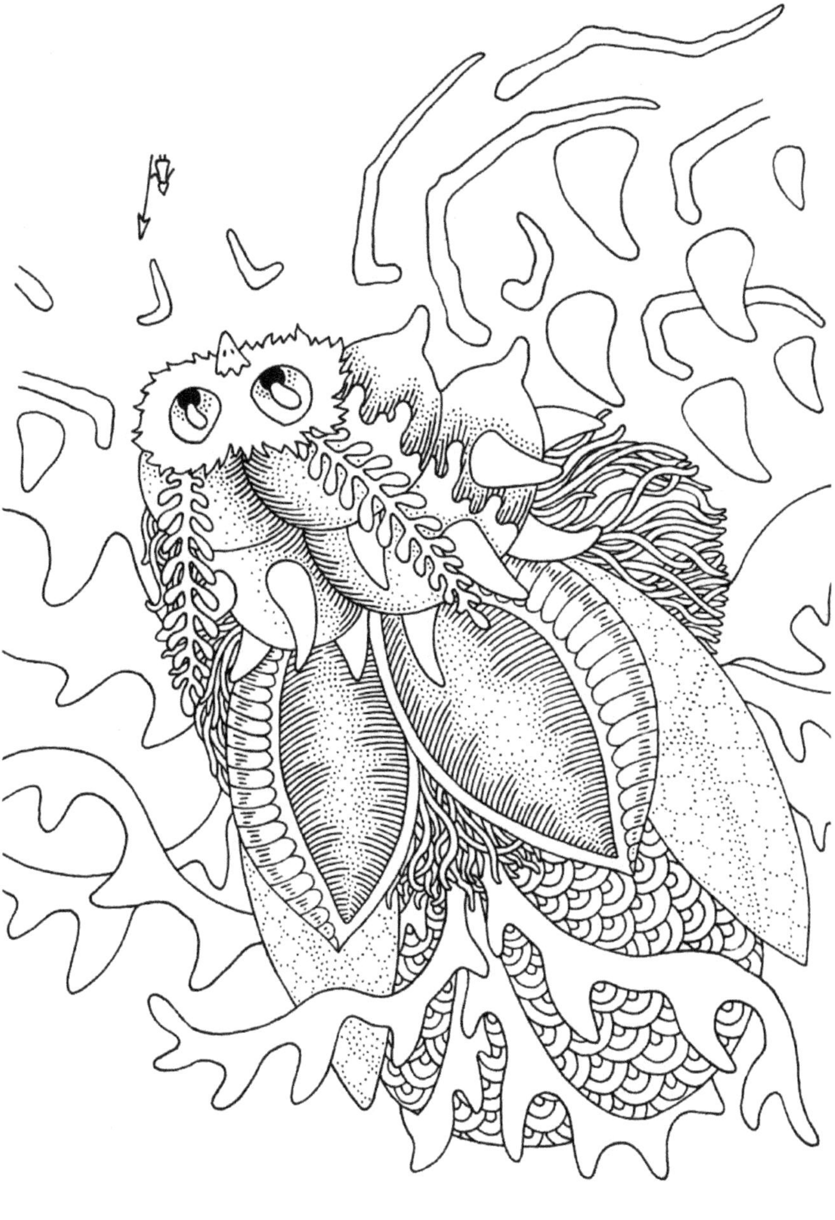

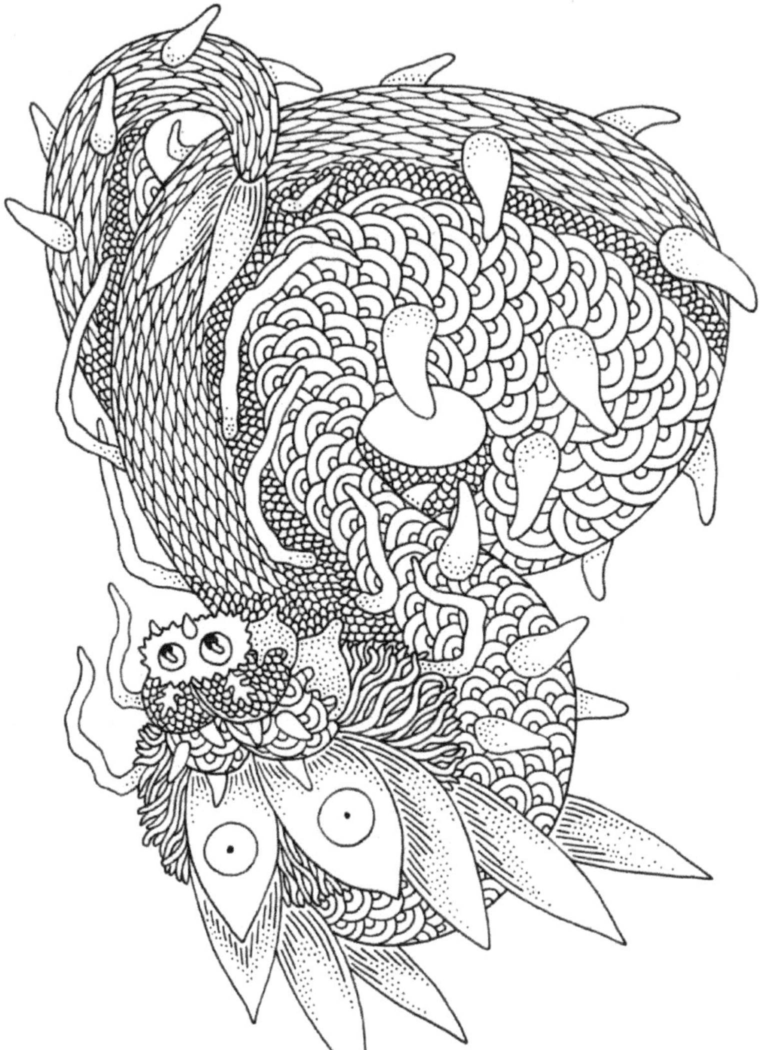

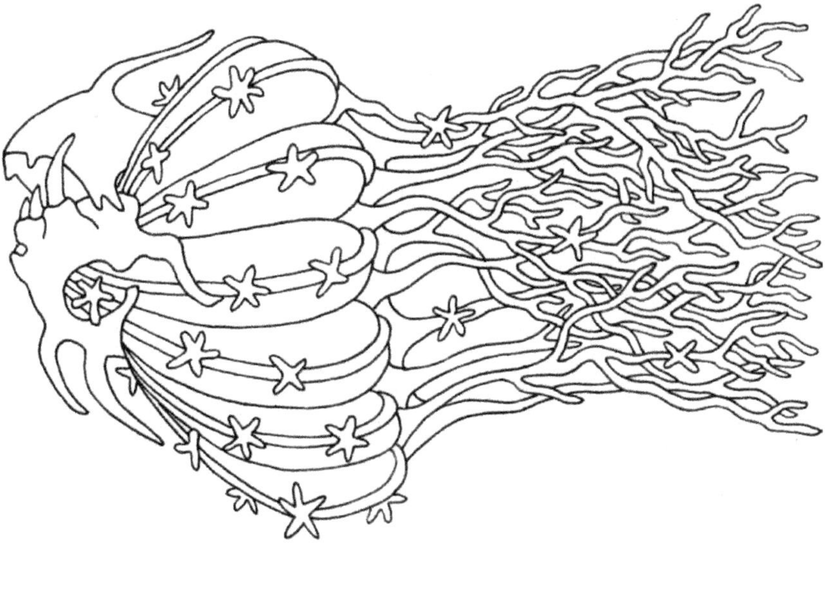

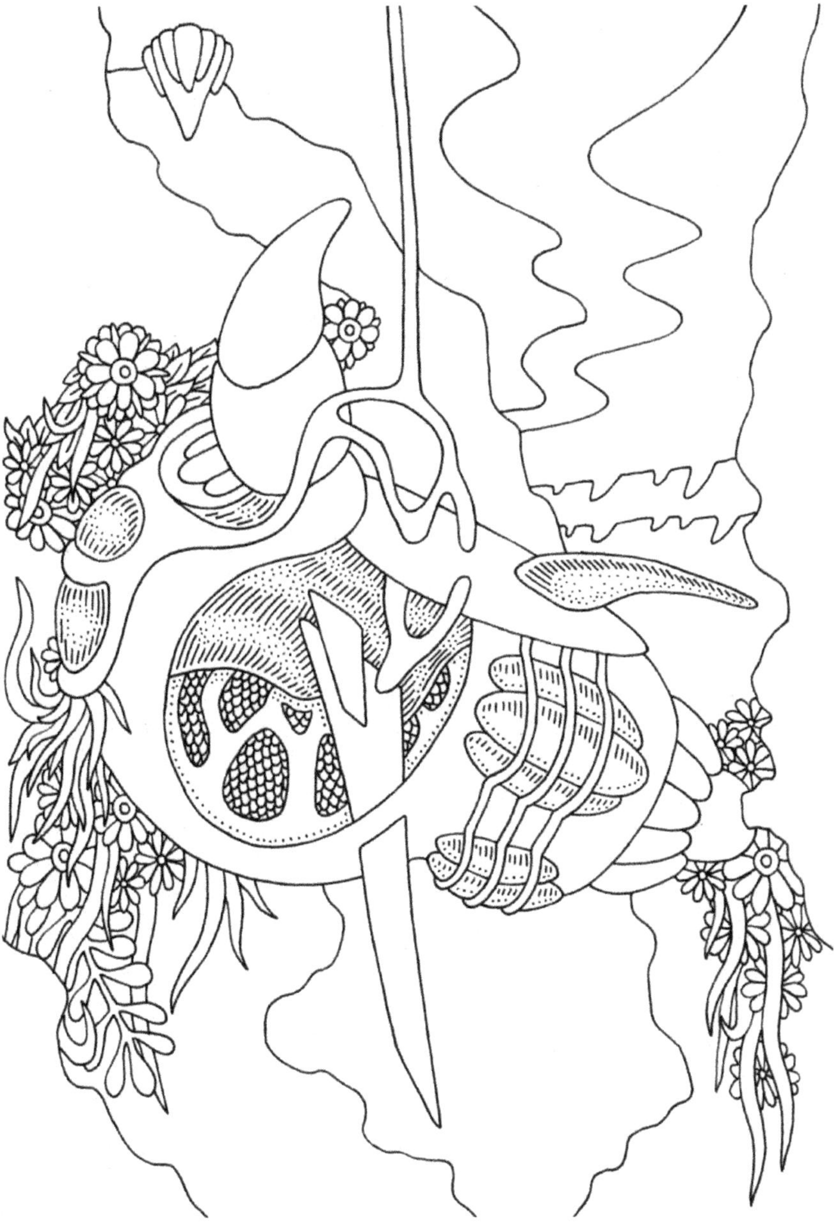

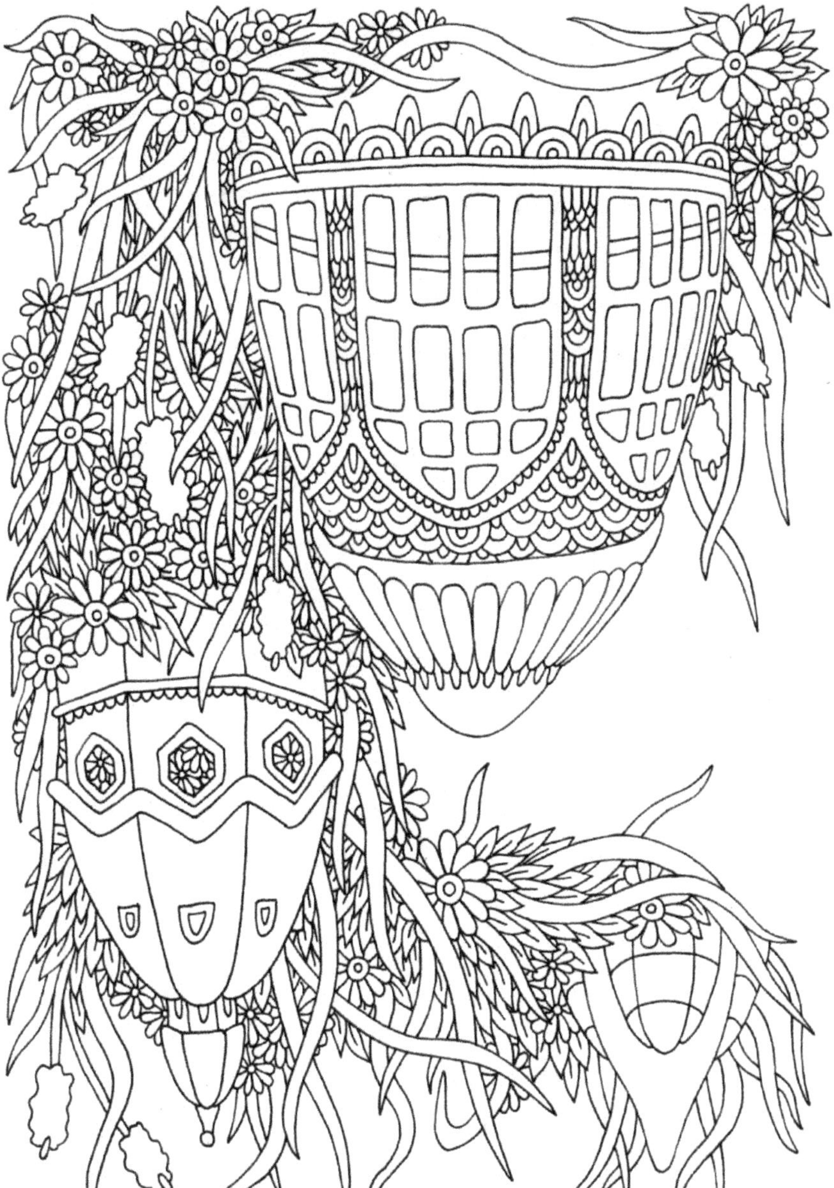

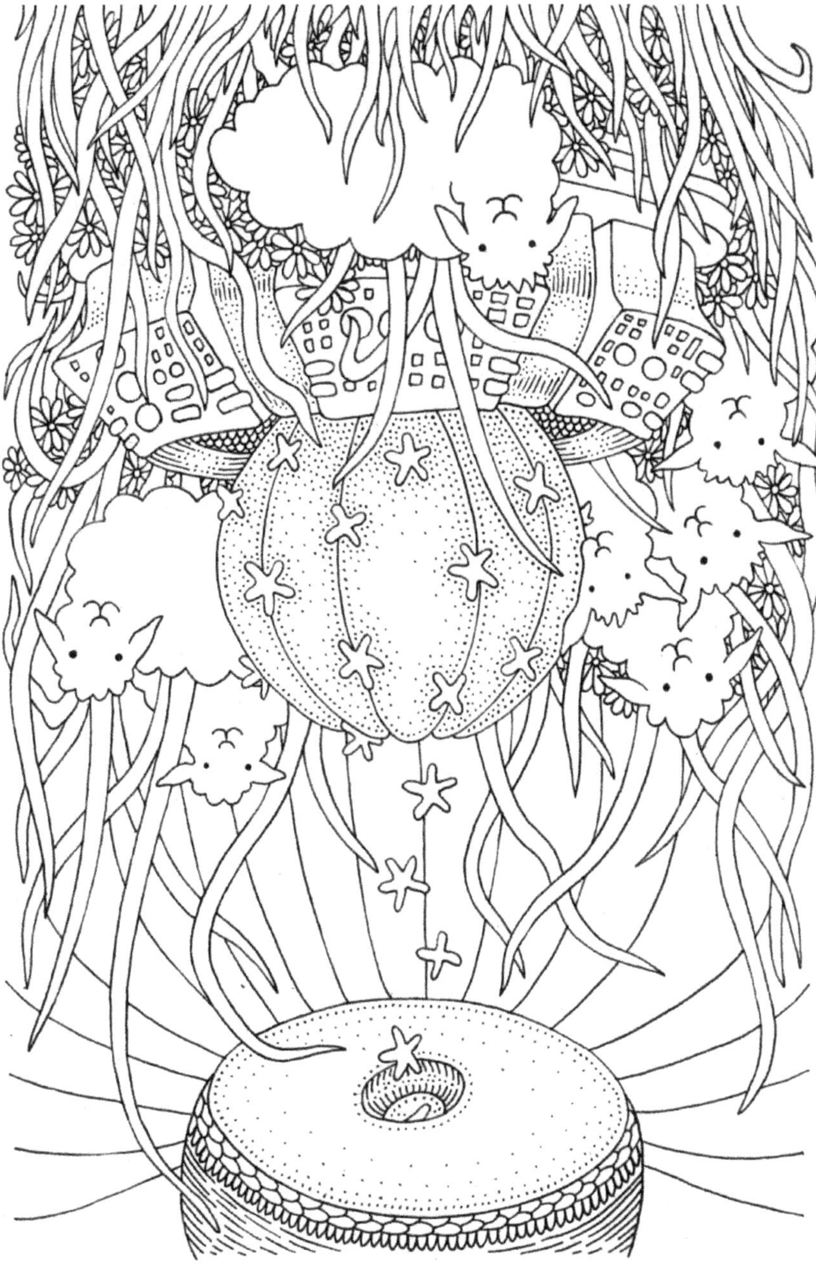

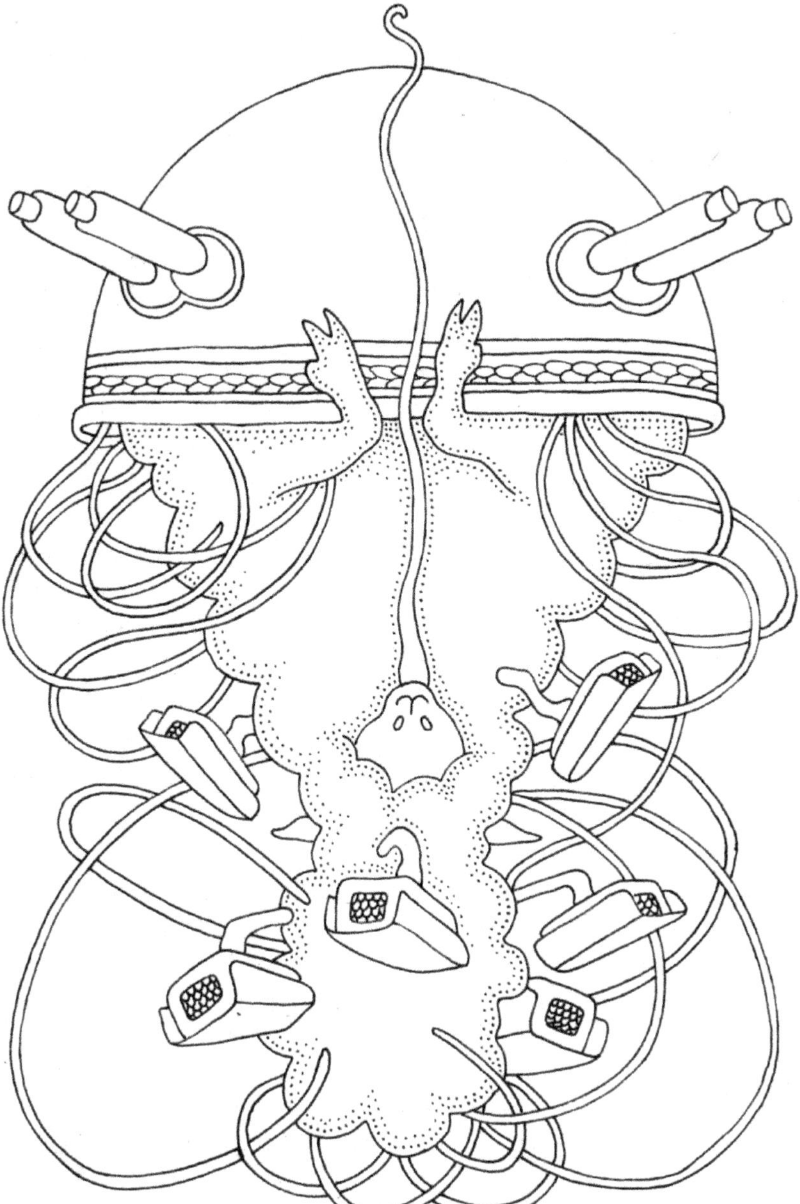

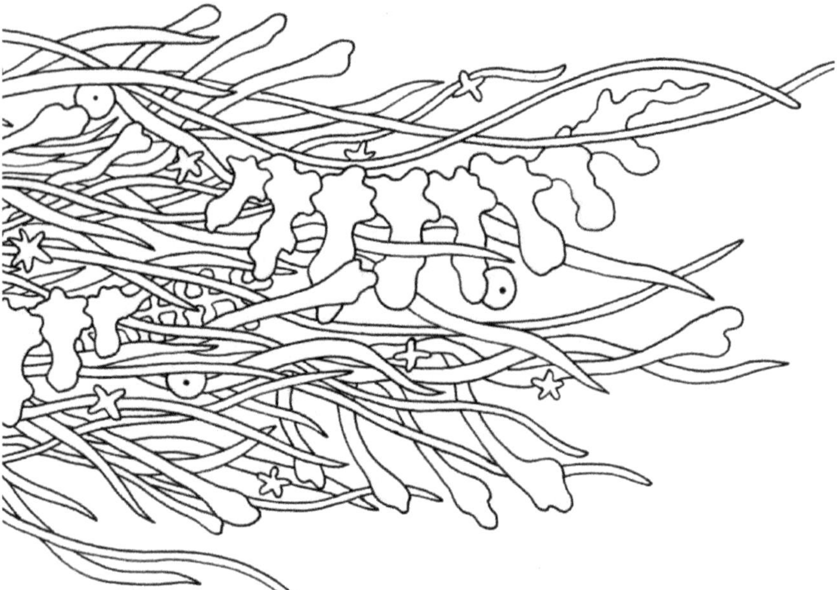

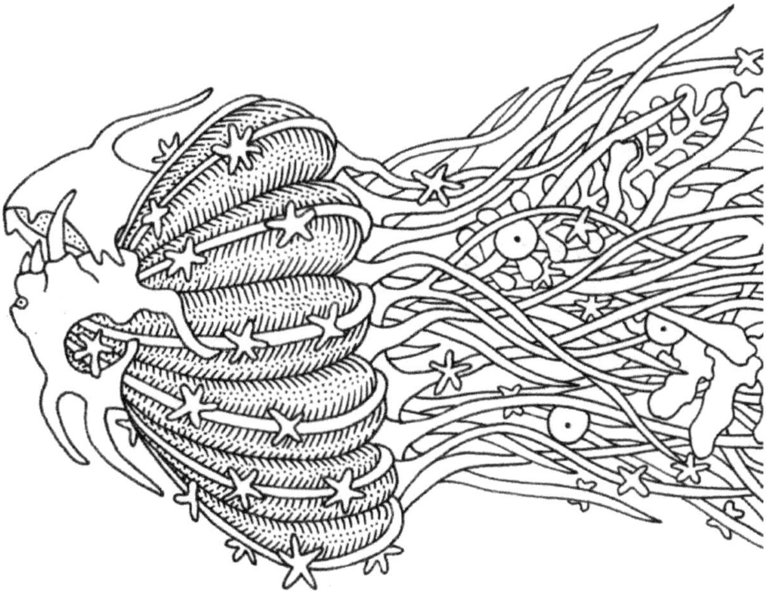

www.ingramcontent.com/pod-product-compliance
Lightning Source LLC
Chambersburg PA
CBHW070849220526
45466CB00005B/1943
* 9 7 8 1 6 5 3 5 5 7 0 4 2 *